Table of
Contents

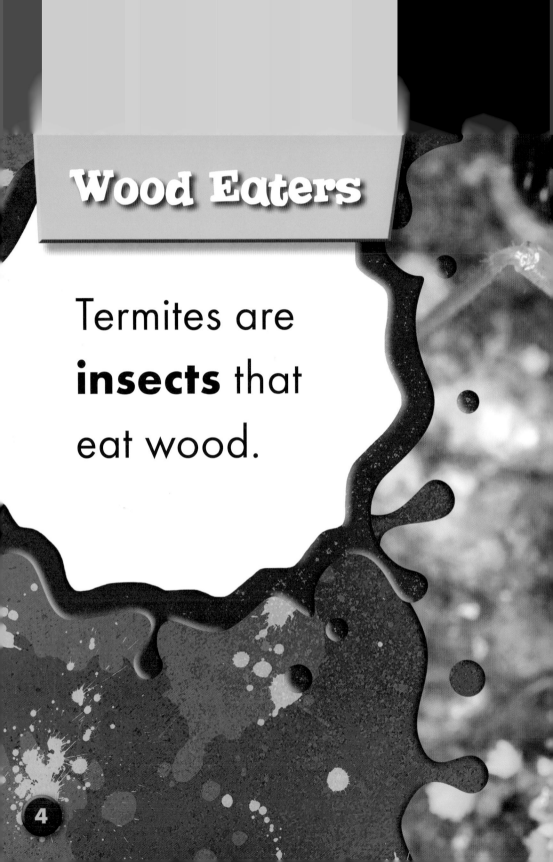

Wood Eaters

Termites are **insects** that eat wood.

CREEPY CRAWLIES

Termites

by Kari Schuetz

BLASTOFF! READERS

BELLWETHER MEDIA • MINNEAPOLIS, MN

Note to Librarians, Teachers, and Parents:

Blastoff! Readers are carefully developed by literacy experts and combine standards-based content with developmentally appropriate text.

Level 1 provides the most support through repetition of high-frequency words, light text, predictable sentence patterns, and strong visual support.

Level 2 offers early readers a bit more challenge through varied simple sentences, increased text load, and less repetition of high-frequency words.

Level 3 advances early-fluent readers toward fluency through increased text and concept load, less reliance on visuals, longer sentences, and more literary language.

Level 4 builds reading stamina by providing more text per page, increased use of punctuation, greater variation in sentence patterns, and increasingly challenging vocabulary.

Level 5 encourages children to move from "learning to read" to "reading to learn" by providing even more text, varied writing styles, and less familiar topics.

Whichever book is right for your reader, Blastoff! Readers are the perfect books to build confidence and encourage a love of reading that will last a lifetime!

This edition first published in 2016 by Bellwether Media, Inc.

No part of this publication may be reproduced in whole or in part without written permission of the publisher. For information regarding permission, write to Bellwether Media, Inc., Attention: Permissions Department, 5357 Penn Avenue South, Minneapolis, MN 55419.

Library of Congress Cataloging-in-Publication Data

Schuetz, Kari, author.
  Termites / by Kari Schuetz.
    pages cm. – (Blastoff! Readers. Creepy Crawlies)
  Summary: "Developed by literacy experts for students in kindergarten through grade three, this book introduces termites to young readers through leveled text and related photos"– Provided by publisher.
  Audience: Ages 5-8
  Audience: K to grade 3
  Includes bibliographical references and index.
  ISBN 978-1-62617-228-9 (hardcover: alk. paper)
  1. Termites–Juvenile literature. I. Title.
  QL529.S35 2016
  595.7'36–dc23
                              2015005964

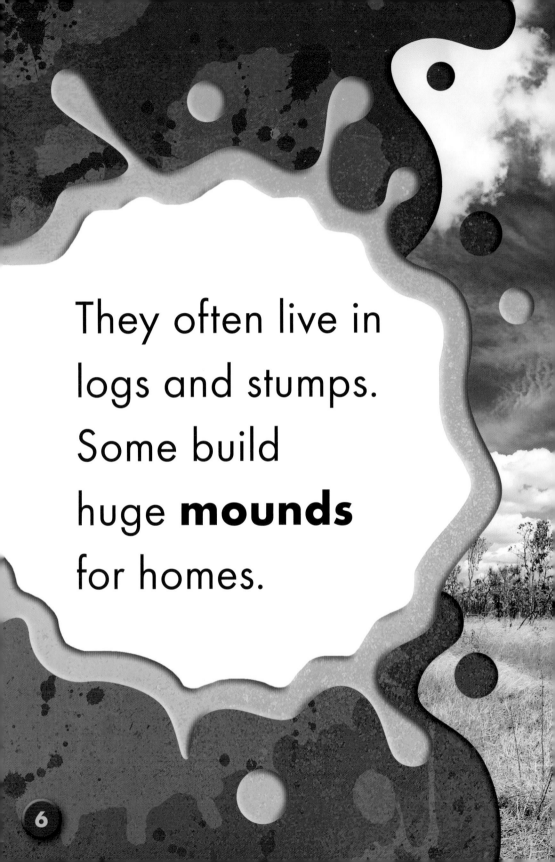

They often live in logs and stumps. Some build huge **mounds** for homes.

mound

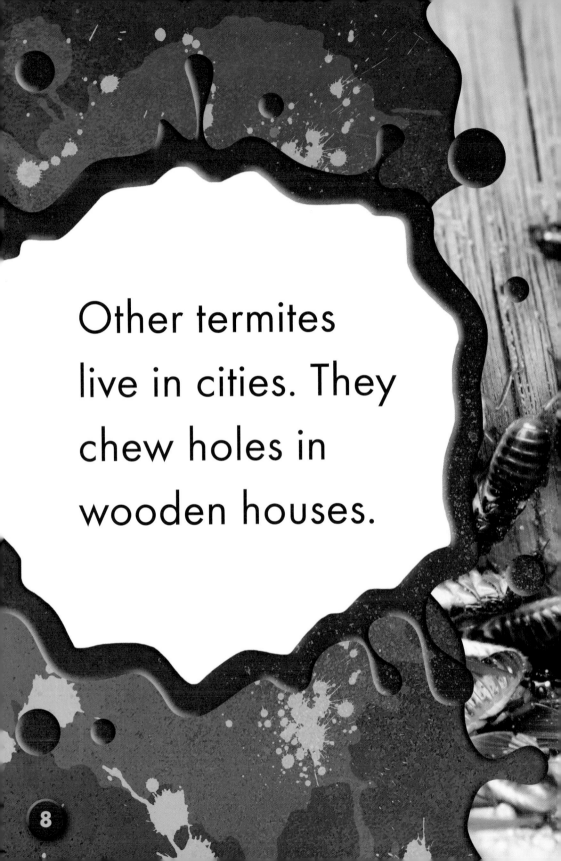

Other termites live in cities. They chew holes in wooden houses.

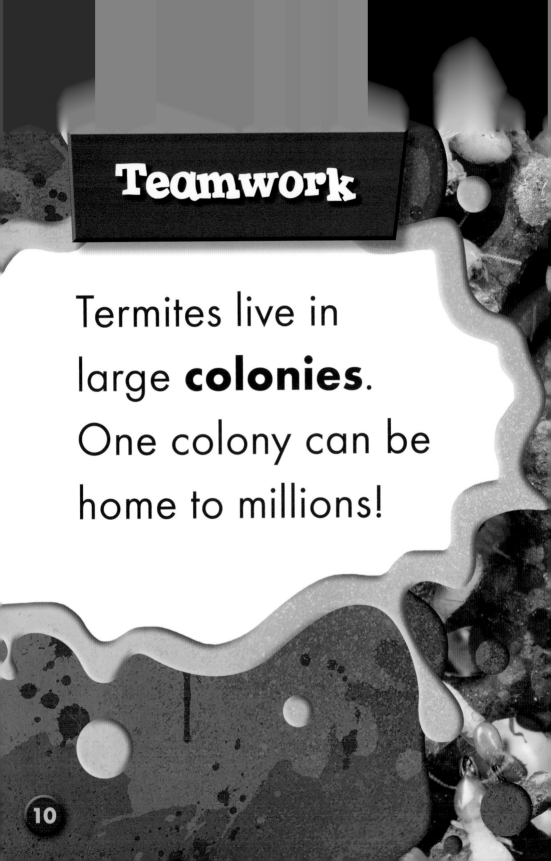

Teamwork

Termites live in large **colonies**. One colony can be home to millions!

Every termite has a job in the colony. Most are **workers**.

workers

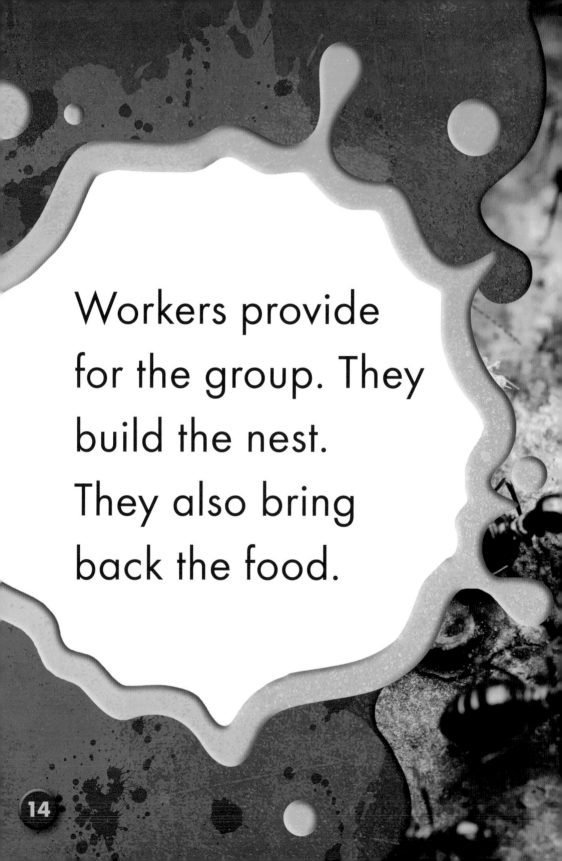

Workers provide for the group. They build the nest. They also bring back the food.

Soldiers protect the nest. They attack outsiders!

soldier

The Royal Family

The **king** and **queen** are the parents of the colony. Their babies are **larvae**.

king

queen

Some larvae grow up to be **swarmers**. They leave to start new colonies!

swarmer

Glossary

colonies—groups of termites that live together

insects—small animals with six legs and hard outer bodies; an insect's body is divided into three parts.

king—the male termite that is the father in the colony

larvae—baby termites

mounds—piles of ground where termites live

queen—the female termite that is the mother in the colony

soldiers—termites that protect the colony from danger

swarmers—termites that leave the colony to start new colonies; swarmers have wings.

workers—termites that build the colony's home and gather food

To Learn More

AT THE LIBRARY

Bodden, Valerie. *Termites*. Mankato, Minn.: Creative Education, 2013.

George, Lynn. *Termites: Mound Builders*. New York, N.Y.: PowerKids Press, 2011.

Porter, Esther. *Termites*. North Mankato, Minn.: Capstone Press, 2014.

ON THE WEB

Learning more about termites is as easy as 1, 2, 3.

1. Go to www.factsurfer.com.

2. Enter "termites" into the search box.

3. Click the "Surf" button and you will see a list of related web sites.

With factsurfer.com, finding more information is just a click away.

Index

The images in this book are reproduced through the courtesy of: Pan Xunbin, front cover (large, small); sydeen, p. 5; Piotr Gatlik, p. 7; bierchen, p. 9; smuay, p. 11; Atthawut, p. 13; Minden Pictures/ SuperStock, pp. 15, 17; Raymond Mendez/ Age Fotostock, p. 19; Dr. Morley Read, p. 21.